Fearless
Public Speaking

2501 01

Donn Rochlin

PublishAmerica
Baltimore

First printing

PublishAmerica has allowed this work to remain exactly as the author intended, verbatim, without editorial input.

ISBN: 1-60813-946-8
PUBLISHED BY PUBLISHAMERICA, LLLP
www.publishamerica.com
Baltimore

Printed in the United States of America

Fearless
Public
Speaking

A woman who survived cancer revealed, in an interview, that she would "rather go through chemo again than speak in public."

A successful businessman considered getting into a car accident the morning he was scheduled to give a group presentation at his company.

There are numerous stories like these relating the stress, fear and panic experienced by millions of individuals who would rather suffer at anything than speak in public.

There are deep psychological factors underlying all fears. This booklet does not attempt to address these factors, but rather to offer an alternate model that I have used with clients and students to drastically reduce their fear of speaking in public. If you at some point choose to research your fears at a deeper level, I believe your research will only enhance the concepts presented here.

This booklet is intended to help you look into some of the causes of your fear of public speaking, and pose some solutions that can help you become aware of where your fear originates, and how to change the way you view public speaking.

Regardless of the size of the group you are addressing, your topic, or personal background, speaking does not have to cause you debilitating fear.

The two primary causes of fear of speaking are perfectionism and performance anxiety. They inhibit and restrict our full potential to realize the fulfillment we long for in our business and personal lives.

Much of the stress and anxiety we feel about speaking before others is the result of our self-imposed demand that our presentations be perfect. As a result, our perfectionism becomes allied with our performance anxiety. They are two sides of the same coin. Once perfectionism and performance anxiety are put into perspective, our energy can flow freely, and our authentic self-expression emerge.

Most people have a preconceived notion of what public speaking involves, and it thus makes sense that they fear it.

Their preconceived notion goes something like this:

You prepare yourself to stand up in front of a group of people (usually unknown to you), impart information, follow an agenda, hope you can field questions intelligently, and, if you're lucky, perhaps pull off a few jokes. You do this all the while having to look professional as your heart is racing, the sweat is rolling off your forehead, and you are silently praying that people like you, especially the people paying you. This scenerio is guaranteed to keep you in a perpetual state of apprehension.

I call this model the Talking Head Syndrome.

TALKING HEAD SYNDROME

If you have ever experienced what I call "death by lecture," you have experienced what the majority of people refer to as public speaking. Most of us think of public speaking as being "talked at" or "lectured to."

I refer to the presenters of this method as "Talking Heads."

TALKING HEADS

A talking head leaves most people feeling bored (uninvolved), tired (uninvolved), and overwhelmed (too much to digest). Talking heads alienate their audience, and create feelings of exhaustion, anxiety, and stress for themselves.

As a talking head, we feel it is our job to "carry the show," to entertain, to be the expert, and to hold ourselves personally responsible for everyone's experience. After all, we want to be well thought of long after our speech is over, and perhaps be asked back. In this paradigm you talk, and they listen (you hope).

In place of the stereotypical model of the talking head, I will redefine public speaking so that you can approach it with more creativity, clarity, and freedom from fear.

LEARNER DRIVEN MODEL

To be an effective, skillful and successful speaker it is absolutely necessary to shift from being a talking head to taking on the role of educator.

It is not how well you know your topic, it's how well you relay your topic to others and how well you activate learning.

The word education is synonymous with the word Educe, which is derived from two Latin roots e, (out) and ducere, (lead), to draw out, to elicit from. This definition of education means to train or impart knowledge by activating students (audiences) so they are participating in the learning process.

It is important to understand as an educator that the combined wisdom of the group is greater than the individual.

By keeping in mind that we are educators, we shift the fear, self-judgment and obsessive worry to an attitude of being in service.

When you are truly in service (heart centered), you cannot focus on fear, which is (ego based).

Think about it!

If a child asks for you help tying their shoes, do you panic and obsess about your qualifications? Do you worry if you are too fat or too thin or funny enough, or if you have perfect diction? No! You jump in and help, because you have something to offer and you are focused on giving it.

Now this may sound simplistic, but what is the difference between a child who needs their shoes tied, or someone who needs leadership skills, or

Insurance, or a new car? You are there to help, and your job involves finding out how you can be of better service and get the persons you are helping what they want and need.

The key is to remember that it's all about them, and you DO NOT have to be the expert, only the conduit. We will touch on this in the upcoming sections of the booklet.

THE THREE KEYS

The three fundamental keys to successful speaking are:

TRANSPARENCY

As a member of the National Speakers Association, I receive the monthly NSA magazine, which is accompanied by a CD. The magazine and CD are filled with interesting and inspiring articles and interviews. Without exception, there is always a reference to the most commonly agreed upon attribute of successful speakers.

More important than a sizzling sense of humor, perfect diction, good looks, impeccable preparation, or expertise on your topic, is the ability to be transparent.

Transparency means letting people see you for who you are. It means being real, being vulnerable with all of your imperfections, standing in your power as you. This quality is extremely attractive because it relaxes, disarms, and creates a bridge to your audience.

Ironically and seemingly contradictory to what was mentioned earlier about focusing on your audience, not you, transparency is all about you.

To be yourself you need to reveal your self. Revealing yourself can be practiced in a number of ways that draw on your personal resources.

STORIES

The power of your personal story gives you instant credibility and respect from your audience. It says to them, I have been there, I have experienced, and I have felt that too. Particularly effective are stories which highlight your defining moments as they relate to your topic (this is discussed later in the Template for Success section). This could include what inspired you to create your topic, how you fell into your current circumstances, or stories about your experiences with mentors, heroes (mythological or real), and inspirational events that encouraged you on your journey.

VULNERABILITY

Be willing to make mistakes under fire. Learn to accept that mistakes are part of the gig. The more you can accept this and relax into the reality of it, the less performance pressure (fear) you will experience.

"The greatest mistake you can make in life is to be continually fearing you will make one."
Elbert Hubbart

It's not about being perfect and not making mistakes, it's about flowing with the so-called mistakes. As the jazz great Miles Davies said, "Man... There are no wrong notes." This is a great metaphor for public speaking, because it encourages creativity and innovation within an existing structure, leaving room for original expression and creativity.

The willingness to be vulnerable is actually an act of courage and, again, shows the human side of you, which, at it's worst, is admirable. I recently saw a great example of the willingness to be vulnerable on a public television tribute to Paul Simon. An all star group of famous singer songwriters, including Stevie Wonder and James Taylor, were assembled to sing Paul Simons songs. They were trading off singing verses. When it came to Stevie Wonder, he forgot the verse and the band had to start over. Without missing a beat Stevie said, "I'm sorry, I couldn't see the cue cards."

One of the greatest contemporary pianists of all time, Vladimir Horowitz, was performing an impeccable and brilliant concert at Carnegie Hall. To the shock and surprise of the critics, he struck the final note of the well known piece he was playing, a note which was not written in the score. When interviewed by the press about this unimaginable folly, his only comment was, "Yes! But I did it with panache!"

The point made so clear in these examples is that

there is no perfection, only a perfect response to imperfection, which is go with the flow, be honest, and embrace your vulnerability.

PREPARE TO IMPROVISE

"How do I proceed? ...I grope."
Albert Einstein

Improvisation (to produce without previous thought or preparation) is a direct descendant of transparency, as it calls upon your ability to be yourself in the face of unplanned events and circumstances.

Regardless of how well prepared and organized you may be going into a presentation, there will always be an opportunity to improvise. As scary as this might sound, it is actually a blessing since improvisation keeps your presentation real and in the moment. Every audience is different and you are different every day. By being too rigid and demanding of yourself, you can easily fall prey to perfectionist thinking and performance anxiety.

Just like in jazz, the freedom to improvise is a by product of being familiar enough with the structure or rules of the music that you can break the rules and create new ideas outside of the box.

In the context of speaking, improvisation can be as simple as using a new metaphor to make a point, or changing the order of your ideas. You can call on an audience member to give an example that will help clarify your point, spontaneously state a new idea or frame your example in a new way, but most of all relax and let the ideas come to you.

Have fun! Love what you are doing; love what you are talking about. Fun is contagious. If you have fun, your audience will too.

ENERGY

$E=mc^2$

In addition to his contribution to the world of quantum physics, Einstein indirectly made a profound contribution to public speaking. I heard a speaker once reconfigure his historic equation $E= mc^2$ to make a point about the importance of connecting with your audience. "Energy = (m) meaningful (c) connection squared (multiplied).

Given that being a speaker is about being an educator, we can view energy as that which relays education in the most profound way. Education is like an arrow aimed at its target, while energy is like the bow, providing the thrust and power to land the arrow precisely.

By relaying our message with energy, we connect in a meaningful way that can make a dramatic impact. An environment filled with enthusiasm, curiosity, and play is an environment where learning can thrive.

The good news is that you don't have to come up with all this energy yourself. Much of the energy you need will come from your audience, as will be discussed later. Because energy is contagious, once you establish your enthusiasm and interest in your topic, the group will add their own energy.

By speaking from enthusiasm, you automatically motivate and inspire. The word enthusiasm is derived from the Greek root "enthous" (inspired, possessed). Because of your genuine connection to your topic, you will always be an inspiration. Your contribution is that of the highest calling. The greatest teachers are those that leave their audience with hope and rekindle their imagination.

To guarantee the highest output of energy, you need to be able to answer yes to these three questions:

Are you genuinely aligned and enthusiastic about your topic(s)?

Do you have the conviction to carry your message to others?

Do you live by example the message that you are imparting?

ENERGY SHIFTERS

Use music whenever possible, as it is an excellent way of creating energy. Have music on when people are being seated. Music diverts what can be the solemn experience of entering into a room full of unknown faces into a welcoming experience.

Have the music on at a low to medium volume, and choose instrumental music only, because people tend to get distracted by lyrics. High-energy music is a good choice as people are adjusting to the room, and also when returning from a break. Soft music can also be used during any written, contemplative exercises. Obviously, it is not possible to use music in every situation. For example, music is not appropriate for short talks such as keynote luncheons. Therefore, "prepare to improvise."

GRATITUDE

Taking a few minutes before people begin to arrive to express gratitude is an excellent way to raise your energy. Be grateful for the experience you are about to have, the connection that you will bring about, and the lives that you will affect. Take a few minutes to stand in front of the room, take a few breaths, and feel the the gratitude for being in the position you are in.

SELF-TALK

"You're gonna make me give myself a good talk'n to!"

Bob Dylan

Sometimes we just need to talk to ourselves to get psyched! One of the traits of champion athletes and performers is the ability to self-coach, using aphorisms, positive visualizations, or just a good old fashion kick in the pants.

One of the most powerful prefaces to any statement is:

I am!

I am going to have an amazing experience here.

I am a successful speaker.

I am contributing to the success of others.

GROUP LEVERAGE

Learning to leverage the energy, wisdom, and enthusiasm of your audience is the most important of the three keys. It is by experiencing how to orchestrate and conduct a group that you begin to obtain a sense of ease and fearlessness about speaking.

In his wonderful book, From Good to Great, Jim Collins writes about the 11 most successful companies in the United States and highlights several of the principles common to their success. One interesting fact was that the CEO's of these companies are rarely household names, and most are not known to the general public. He makes the point that these leaders have learned how to subjugate their egos to the greater good, demonstrating that it is the collective wisdom, resources, and energy of the members of their company that is responsible for the success of the organization.

An example of how the companies use collective wisdom is in the way many of them conduct their meetings. Using a model based on "Open Space Technology," meetings are conducted in an open participation format, where all employees are invited to share their views and offer suggestions. One such company earned dividends amounting to millions of dollars based on a suggestion from a janitor, whose perspective was not obvious from the position of middle or upper management.

Regardless of the length or nature of a presentation, there is always an opportunity to leverage the wisdom of the group.

Get them doing stuff !

Memorize this truth: The less you do, the more successful you will be! Ironic as it may sound, you need to train yourself to relinquish control of every aspect of your presentation, and get them to do stuff!

The following are six steps that when followed will help you feel less stressed out about public speaking, and thus confident. In addition, these steps will help you feel respected and appreciated by your audience.

1. THE ICE BREAKER

Let's face it, sometimes it can feel extremely intimidating to walk into a room full of people whom you don't know, and who also don't know you and each other.

The very first thing I do when the clock strikes "starting time" is to casually stroll up to the front of the room and announce something like this :

While we're waiting to get started, and just to get to

know each other a little bit better, I would like you to find a partner (someone you did not come with), and take about four minutes to share with your partner:

why you are here

what you would like to get out of this presentation

What's great about this step is it immediately warms up the room, and creates a space for people to share (before you have uttered a word about your topic). The audience feel less intimidated and more relaxed about what is going to take place. You'll also find that because they are engaged with each other and not focused on you, you can breath easier. I use this time to sort out notes, do a little breathing, and scan the room, sometimes just taking the time to be grateful to be in the position I'm in and for all the people contributing to my employment.

2. ENROLLING QUESTIONS

Ask enrolling questions at the conclusion of the ice breaker. Enrolling questions are questions related to the topic of your talk. They help the audience become involved or "enrolled" in your talk, and establish an energetic tone for your presentation. Asking enrolling questions raises the energy of the group because it reminds people that you are there for them and establishes a common ground. Examples of enrolling questions are:

How many of you have experienced "death by lecture?"

How many of you have an experience or topic you are passionate about that you feel others could learn from?This type of questioning gets people nodding their heads in agreement and directs their energy to where you are going. They thus become "enrolled" in the experience.

3. REVIEWING AGENDA

In this step you ask for a volunteer to come up and write down the answers to the questions asked in the ice breaker. If the class is over a dozen people, pick about six people to report on why their team member is here, and what they would like to get out of the class. By asking team members to talk about each other, you are reinforcing team participation as well as subtly reminding people that you expect them to pay attention.

Another benefit to this step is that by being willing to listen to people's reasons for attending, you are establishing that it is your intent to give them what they want, not simply a one size fits all presentation.

Most people will answer more or less in the same way. For example, if your presentation topic is how to be a fearless public speaker, they will say they want to get over their fear of speaking, that they want to be a more effective and persuasive speaker, that they want to learn how to engage the audience, and that they want to learn how to have more confidence in front of people (all basically the same issues) in order to become a better speaker.

You have assured them in your description of your topic that that is what they will get. Your audience is not really concerned with how you deliver this information as long as they feel that they are receiving value and their concerns are acknowledged. All covered in this step!

4. DRINK TEA!

Years ago I had a teacher who taught me what I consider to be one of the great teachings of a successful speaker: "Drink Tea."

What drinking tea means is to have the audience participate in your presentation as much as possible, as you quietly retreat to a corner of the stage and sip on your tea. Because true learning is an interactive experience, the more they do the more successful you are.

For example:

Except for writing your name on the flip chart, never write anything yourself.

a. When setting the agenda, have a volunteer come up and be your scribe. Any point that you want to emphasize in writing, have someone come up and do the writing for you.

b. Never directly answer a question. This is an amazing technique but one you will probably need to work on, since your tendency will be to jump in as the "teacher" and field the question. Simply ask, who would like to answer that?

Then slip off and sip some tea.

After the question has been answered, ask, "Who would like to comment on that?" (as you go sip tea.) Here is where you put any bias or need for a correct answer on hold.

It is not about a right or wrong answer as much as it is about "possible" answers. Again, if you let go of the role of expert and embrace the role of facilitator you will be more effective.

c. Depending on the length of your presentation, there will be one or more opportunities for you to initiate some team exercises, at which time you can go refill your tea cup.

More on this later.

d. Another fun way to involve the group is to periodically tear off your notes from the flip chart and have people tape them to the wall (giant sticky notes are available for this purpose). Before a break, have people team up and go around the room and explain the notes to each other. Sharing in this way with each other reinforces the information and gives the team members an opportunity to teach it back to someone else.

THE TEMPLATE FOR SUCCESS

ICE BREAKER
TWO ENROLLING QUESTIONS
WELCOME/NAME/NAME OF TALK
ACKNOWLEDGE AUDIENCE/THANK SPONSER
WIIFM (WHAT'S IN IT FOR ME?)
GET PERMISSION/YOUR RIGHT TO BE
DATA
DATA EXERCISE/PS/CS
BOOKSTORE

ICE BREAKER: To recap, the icebreaker is done as soon as the class is scheduled to begin. Have people find a partner, team up and ask A. What motivated you to attend this class (presentation)? B. What would you like to take home? Put a 5-minute time limit on the sharing.

TWO ENROLLING QUESTIONS: Make these short and concise! For example: How many of you have ever been terrified to speak in public. Raise your hand if you have ever considered changing careers because you were afraid to give speeches. Remember, the idea here is to get people in agreement with your topic by relating it to their experience and interest regarding your topic.

WELCOME/NAME/NAME OF TALK... This is pretty straight forward!

Simply welcome the audience, and give your name and the name of the talk.

ACKNOWLEDGE AUDIENCE/THANK SPONSER

Thank the audience for being there. I usually say something like "I appreciate you being here today so that I get to go to work and do what I love." Or, "thank you for the opportunity to share a topic near and dear to me."

Thank sponsor. Thank those who have made it possible for you to be where you are, even if it is just the organization you rented the room from.

WIIFM: WHAT'S IN IT FOR ME?

With this step you highlight the main benefits that the audience will gain from your presentation, including the psychological, and technical benefits.

For example, say: you will discover why most people are afraid of speaking in front of groups.

You will learn three of the most important ingredients for successful speaking.

You will gain confidence by learning how to make a few simple changes in how you present yourself.

You will learn how to save time...
You will save money...
You will have less frustration and stress...
You will feel more confident...
Whatever applies to your topic, summarize the benefits to your audience.

ASK PERMISSION/THE RIGHT TO BE
Always ask permission to share your right to be. (your qualifications) This is a very subtle but powerful step. By asking permission and not imposing this step on people, they will feel acknowledged rather than held captive. Most speakers do not use this step, and thus risk alienating their audience right from the start.

Even if people are thinking, no, I don't want to hear about you, they will feel respected and acknowledged. (I've never experienced anyone saying no!)

With this step you are projecting the image of yourself as qualified and experienced enough to speak about the topic. It is extremely important not to hold back, but to assert your credentials, your experiences and your passion, in other words, your right to be teaching this information. First, briefly explain why you are sharing this information. This is where a short story pertaining to your connection with the topic will command attention, i.e., "I started teaching group piano over 15 years ago and was always meeting such interesting and creative people, that I thought how many people would love to be doing what I'm doing, giving seminars and workshops about something that they love to do while reaping the emotional, spiritual, and financial rewards? So I got the idea of showing others what I have learned over the years and how they can do the same thing within their area of expertise. Since that time I have given presentations and trainings at colleges, universities and businesses in over 56 cities, and have had the opportunity to help thousands of people enjoy the benefits of public speaking and teaching."

People respond to statistics. How long have you been doing what you are doing? Do you have degrees, certifications, etc.? How many people have you taught? Who and what are you inspired by? The point is to make yourself big, not in an egotistical way but in a way that informs your audience that you are qualified to be in front of them.

Even if you are just starting out, don't have degrees, credentials or even a lot of experience, highlight what you do have even if it's a string of seeming "failures." Great! You failed your way to success. How many stories have people heard of great baseball legends that have held as many strike out records as home run records? The point is we are inspired by the fact that they got up to bat so often, and hung in there. You can always make up for a deficit of credentials and documentation by expressing passion for your topic...i.e., since I was three years old I have loved to...

There's nothing I would rather do than...

I have spent every spare weekend doing...

Passion is energy and gives you immediate credibility.

Keep this step short and concise (4 to 5 minutes).

DATA

Data: Facts and figures through which conclusions are drawn. This step is the body of your presentation, where you will be delivering the goods and clarifying the challenges and solutions that are inherent in your topic Remember relax, you don't have to do this on your own. The energy of the group will guide you.

The first step is to "State Your Case." You can refer back to the enrolling question that you asked early on:

How many of you are panic stricken when it comes to public speaking? Well, you're not alone. In a survey it was revealed that 98% of people in business are reluctant to speak in front of groups out of fear of judgment, inadequacies, etc.

How much more productive would you be if you could feel confident speaking in front of groups?

You can use these guidelines in stating your case:

State situation as it is:

Most people fear speaking.

Speaking is a critical skill in business.

The traditional way to remedy this situation has been to learn techniques offered the "Pros" and hope eventually some of it will rub off on you.

Most speakers unfortunately view speaking as talking at their audience and don't know how to leverage the energy and wisdom of the group.

This is a good place to have a volunteer come up and read any quotes or passages that help clarify your message.

Remember that if you're using a dry erase board to make a visual impact, have a volunteer do the writing for you.

TYPES OF EXERCISES

Written exercises: Make a questionnaire with a variety of questions relating to your topic. Have people work individually for 5-10 minutes. For example, have them list their most memorable public speaking experience. You can ask them such questions as: Who are your favorite speakers and why? What do you admire most about good speakers? What are your greatest fears about speaking ?

PARTNER SHARE EXERCISE

Have people team up and share their answers with each other (5-10 minutes). This is a good time to put some quiet music on in the background.

CLASS SHARE

Ask for some volunteers to share what they have written. Always have volunteers stand when addressing the audience. I also suggest asking for a round of applause after everyone has shared, to acknowledge everyone's participation. Exercises of this nature take the focus off of you and stimulate group participation and team learning.

MARKETING

Once you have discovered which topic(s) you are going to present, there are a number of ways to get started as a speaker. For immediate income and to gain confidence and experience, I recommend community education programs. These programs are typically offered through community colleges, school districts, universities and specific business associations.

Start looking into organizations that are closest to you geographically or in cities and towns that you would like to visit.

One of the advantages of teaching through community education is:

1.They do all of the promoting for your class, which

generally includes a listing in their Community Ed catalogue, which is directly mailed to the community.

They provide a classroom or facility for you.
They take registration.

To make this arrangement profitable for you, it is important that you be paid on a percentage basis. Even though many colleges will tell you that they only pay hourly, ask if they would consider working on a contract basis with you.

I have persuaded many colleges to pay me a percentage rather than hourly. If they seem unwilling to do this, ask if they can arrange to pay you:

an honorarium
as a vendor
as a contractor

I don't recommend ever accepting less then 50%, and I receive as much as 80 % from many of my sponsoring schools. Start your negotiations high, keeping in mind your expenses and personal value.

With this arrangement. you can derive as much as three streams of income. The first stream is from the percentage the school pays you. The second is from materials that you buy or have created for resale that will be used in the class.

The next category to be covered later is that of "Add On Products" also know as BOR or "Back Of The Room Sales."

Other venues to consider for your presentation are:

1. Rotary clubs
2. Chamber of commerce groups
3. Professional associations

Many of these groups do not pay, but can be used as a platform to generate sign ups for other workshops and classes that you will be offering.

When approaching these groups, it is important to establish your motive to announce an upcoming workshop class etc. in exchange for your time.

Additionally you can ask for referrals from the participants of other groups or organizations they belong to that might be interested in your topic. You can also leverage your time with pro bono presentations by asking for testimonials. If you are just starting your business, gathering testimonials will really pay off as you start to integrate them into your promotional materials.

Below are samples of

A referral form (to be passed out at the end of your presentation

A testimonial form

Sample:

If you enjoyed today's presentation, I would greatly appreciate the name and contact information of any individual, business, or organization you feel might benefit from my program:

Referral   _____

Contact Information _____

Your name and company / and your affiliation with referral   _____

THANK YOU

You can ask your sponsor if you can pass these out in advance of your presentation, or you can ask for several volunteers at the end of the program to pass out this form and the testimonial form.

SAMPLE
TESTIMONIAL

Name   _____

Occupation   _____

Age _____

City/State   _____

Phone   _____/_____/_____

E/mail   _____

Comments:

_____

_____

_____

THANK YOU!

BACK OF THE ROOM SALES

If you don't have these already, you'll want to create or find additional products that will enhance the information in your presentation. No matter how effective you are as a speaker, people will only retain a small percentage of what you say. Add on products can help people reinforce your information and give them "portable" motivation and inspiration.

Add on products can be in the form of CD's, DVD's books, etc. If you don't have products developed yet, you can affiliate with others who have products that would be beneficial to your audience.

You can Google your topic and see what's out there or simply make calls to the creators of products that you like and work out a wholesale discount. I have been very successful with this method while developing my own products, and still continue several of these relationships.

TIPS FOR BACK OF THE ROOM SALES

Always have help whenever possible. Having a helper take money and do the paper work will free you up to answer questions and allow you be more available for those who want to speak with you.

Always ask permission to announce your add-ons.

My introduction usually goes something like:

How many of agree that it's difficult to retain everything that you hear and experience at a workshop? How many of you agree that no matter how wonderful the class, you still need to practice the information?

Is it okay with you if I take 4 minutes and tell you about the products in the back of the room that are specifically created to help reinforce today's topic, and keep you motivated?
At this point, make several bullet points about each product.

"The book will help you with these five principles."

"The CD will cover the seven keys to success and is convenient to listen to while driving."

"The DVD recaps everything we discussed here today. It's like attending the workshop again as many times as you like."

Remember to ask permission. By honoring people

this way they become more receptive to your offer and won't feel like you just went from being Dr.Jekyll (caring compassionate teacher) to Mr. Hyde (bloodthirsty salesman,) be sincere. You must believe that your add-ons have value and will benefit your audience.

CREATE AN OFFER

I simply say "The normal price for the Books, CD's, etc. on my website is abc, but today ONLY you can get them for xyz. Then stick with the price you give ! Never use the word "discounted." The word discount does just that! It discounts the value of your products at a subconscious level. Instead, say "special pricing."

Have two or three (at the most) buying options
A. The book
B. The book and CD
the book, CD & DVD (master pack)

You might want to find out how to process credit cards, because you can easily add 20% or more to your sales if you have credit card processing capability.

There are two opportunities to announce your BOR offers:
At the conclusion of your presentation, or
At the conclusion of the most powerful part of your

demonstration and just before a break

You can experiment and see what works for you. With shorter presentations, it is generally best to announce these offers at the conclusion of of your program. In a longer presentation, announcing the opportunity midway plants a seed and gives people a little longer to respond to the offer.

SEEDING YOUR PRODUCTS
Seeding means that you refer to the benefits of your product within the context of the presentation.

For example, you can say "There are several techniques on breaking the ice that I will be covering, and these also appear on page 10 of my book."

By doing this you are telling people that the information is available to study and review in a written text which they can take home.

This technique needs to be used subtly. Don't beat people over the head with it. Remember you are there to teach. The BOR sales are important, but you will always do fine financially by being true to your mission. Be in service first.

CONCLUSION

I hope this text has been helpful to you and serves as a guide to an enjoyable and profitable journey into public speaking. There are numerous resources out there to help you refine your craft. I urge you to try on what fits and leave the rest.

Remember...keep it simple and don't overwhelm yourself with details and laborious techniques.

"We never do anything well until we cease to think about the manner of doing it!"
William Hazlitt

Following your intuition allows your true genius and talents to emerge naturally. Love what you are doing—love always conquers fear!

I WISH YOU SUCCESS!

Printed in the United States
220631BV00002B/9/P